HOW TO LIVE WITH A NEUROTIC CAT

Books of similar interest from
Random House Value Publishing:

How to Live with a Neurotic Dog
How to Talk to Your Cat
Cat Tales: Classic Tales from Favorite Authors
Illustrated Catwatching
The Cat Lover's Book of Fascinating Facts
The Personality of the Cat

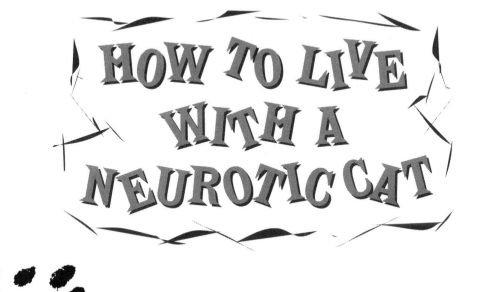

HOW TO LIVE WITH A NEUROTIC CAT

Stephen Baker
with illustrations by Jackie Geyer

Gramercy Books
New York

This 1999 edition is published by Gramercy Books™, an imprint of
Random House Value Publishing, Inc. 201 East 50th Street,
New York, N.Y. 10022, by arrangement with Warner Books/
Bernard Geis Associates, New York

Gramercy Books™ and colophon are trademarks of Random House
Value Publishing, Inc.

Random House
New York • Toronto • London • Sydney • Auckland
http://www.randomhouse.com/

Printed and bound in the United States of America.

Library of Congress Cataloging–in–Publication Data

Baker, Stephen, 1921-
       How to live with a neurotic cat / Stephen Baker ; with
    illustrations by Jackie Geyer.
           p.   cm.
       Originally published: New York : Warner Books, 1985.
       ISBN 0-517-20734-6 (hc)
       1. Cats—Humor.   I. Title.
    PN6231.C23B35   1999
    636.8'02'07—dc21   99-24728
                                                           CIP

8 7 6 5

Designed by Giorgetta Bell McRee

Pawprints by Borris

CONTENTS

INTRODUCTION

And then God created a furry lump which for lack of a better name He called the Cat. He looked at His creation and shook His head. It wasn't exactly what He had in mind.

He held the thing up in the air and it hung limply from His fingers. He dropped it to the ground, and it spread out in all directions as flat as a pancake. And when He crossed the forelegs across the chest and folded the hind legs into a lotus position, that is exactly where the limbs stayed.

His curiosity piqued, He turned the body over, stretching it to almost twice its length. He rolled it into a small ball, twisting, bending, kneading it. The thing did not even open its eyes.

He rubbed His beard incredulously. He didn't know whether to laugh or cry. He knew of course that what He had just created was less than a miracle.

But there was no time to make changes, not with the seven-day deadline just around the corner.

"Oh, well." He shrugged. "You can't win them all."

With not a moment to spare upon its arrival on earth, the cat curled up and went back to sleep.

What Makes a Cat Neurotic? | 1

A recent census taken among cats shows that approximately 100 percent are neurotic. That estimate is probably on the low side.

The reason for their neurosis is simple enough. It's you.

Consider this. Your cat loves everything about you: your living room couch, the food you eat, the bed you sleep on, your television set. He enjoys sharing these things with you. Yet, many owners take up more space on the bed at night than their cat; and change television channels indiscriminately; and refuse to offer a seat to their cat at the dining table.

Modern life makes demands on the cat.

Only the fittest survive today. Here is a typical daily schedule of a cat, trying to cope.

4:30 A.M.	Owner turns around in bed, waking up cat.
5:05 A.M.	Owner, still asleep, pulls the blanket over his head—and the cat's next to him on the pillow. Disturbed by all this activity so early in the morning, cat seeks refuge deep under the blanket.
6:00 A.M.	Owner turns around, flattening cat under his belly. Cat lets out a piercing cry and scratches him.
6:01 A.M.	Cat retracts his claws.

6:02 A.M.	Owner shoves cat off the bed. Cat bounces back like a rubber ball, landing smack on owner's face.
6:30–6:45 A.M.	Owner wipes the blood off his face and tries to go back to sleep.
7:00 A.M.	Cat moves to the far side of the bed, taking most of the blanket with him.
7:30 A.M.	Alarm clock goes off. Cat knocks clock off the night table to stop the noise. Clock keeps ringing. Cat pounces on it. Clock stops ringing. Forever.
7:31 A.M.	Owner staggers to the bathroom. Cat jumps on sink to watch him shave and then on side of the bathtub to see him take a shower. When owner begins to sing, cat promptly leaves in disgust. He returns to bed to catch up on his lost sleep.
7:40 A.M.	Owner puts on his shoes and accidentally sits on cat.
7:41 A.M.	Cat goes back to sleep on the floor. Owner trips over him and falls on his face. Cat follows owner to the living room and goes to sleep on the living room couch.
8:15 A.M.	Owner leaves for work.
9:30 A.M.	Cat wakes up and goes to the kitchen to have breakfast.
9:35 A.M.	Passing his dish, cat jumps up on the kitchen counter, reaches into the cookie jar. Eats one cookie, returns to the living room and goes back to sleep.
12:30 P.M.	Cat pays another visit to the kitchen, to help himself to another cookie.
1:30 P.M.	Cat moves to the windowsill to check out the birds. Satisfied, he returns to the couch.

1:45–2:30 P.M.	Cat sharpens his claws, tearing off what is left of the upholstery. He then digs a hole in the carpet.
2:35 P.M.	Cat goes back to the kitchen for one more cookie.
2:45 P.M.	Cat climbs up the living room curtains for exercise. Exhausted, he goes back to sleep.
6:15 P.M.	Owner returns.
6:20 P.M.	Owner mixes beef and gravy for cat, who will have no part of it.
6:25 P.M.	Owner offers cat fresh Beluga caviar. Cat accepts.
6:40 P.M.	Owner sits down in his easy chair to read the evening paper. Cat parks himself across the center spread.
6:41 P.M.	Owner pushes cat off.
6:42 P.M.	Cat jumps back.
6:43 P.M.	Owner pushes cat off.
6:44 P.M.	Cat jumps back.
6:45 P.M.	Owner pushes cat off and moves to couch hoping for a chance to read his paper.
6:46 P.M.	Cat follows him and jumps in his lap.
6:47 P.M.	Owner pushes cat off.
6:48 P.M.	Cat jumps back, tearing the paper in half.
6:49 P.M.	Owner hurls cat against the wall across the room. Cat lands on the floor and grins.
6:50 P.M.	Cat returns to owner's lap.
6:51 P.M.	Owner gets up and walks to the kitchen to make a sandwich.
6:52 P.M.	Cat clings to his trousers. Owner tries to shake him off. Cat perseveres.

7:15 P.M.	Owner succeeds in separating cat from his trousers. He sits down to watch football on television. Cat jumps on his shoulders, gazing fixedly at owner's pastrami sandwich.
7:16 P.M.	Owner asks: "Want half of my sandwich?"
7:17 P.M.	Cat nods.
7:30 P.M.	Cat watches television for a while, but loses interest in the outcome of the game. He leaves for the bedroom.
10:30 P.M.	Owner joins him.
10:45 P.M.	Cat wakes up and takes position.
11:30 P.M.	Both owner and cat go to sleep, though not necessarily in that order.

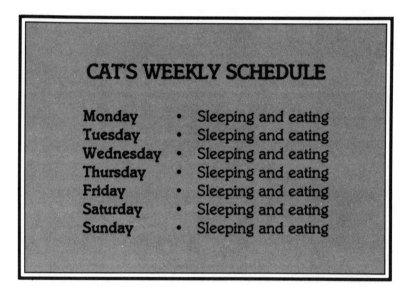

CAT'S WEEKLY SCHEDULE

Monday	• Sleeping and eating
Tuesday	• Sleeping and eating
Wednesday	• Sleeping and eating
Thursday	• Sleeping and eating
Friday	• Sleeping and eating
Saturday	• Sleeping and eating
Sunday	• Sleeping and eating

Kittens are born with their eyes shut. They open them in about six days, take a look around, then close them again for the better part of their natural lives.

The hunting instinct is as basic to a house cat as eating and sleeping or watching television. After all, his is a long line of predatory ancestry, including such fierce a member as the saber-toothed tiger. He knows he has a noble tradition to maintain.

It is indeed an inspiring sight to watch a cat stalking his elusive prey. Nothing escapes his attention. He is poised to deal the mortal blow even if that means putting his own life in jeopardy. His muscles quiver, his tail twitches, his eyes stay affixed. And just at the right moment, he pounces on his victim with unerring instinct, and often in full bloodthirsty cry to the memory of his long-gone relatives in the wild.

His favorite—and sometimes only—big game are: tennis balls, houseplants, goldfish, cigarette butts, ice cubes, your big toe, catnip-impregnated rubber mice, and anything deep down in the garbage can.

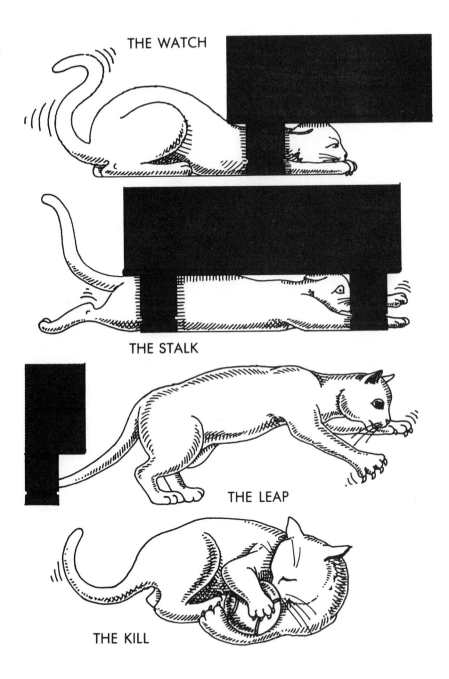

THE WATCH

THE STALK

THE LEAP

THE KILL

A common misconception about cats concerns their intelligence compared to that of other animals. It is said that today's cat no longer needs the jungle smarts of his great grandparents, and thus has grown lazy in his thinking. Not so.

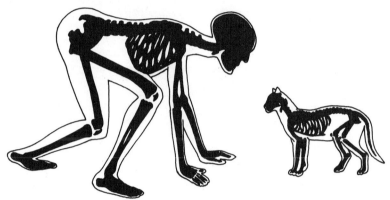

There is strong evidence that cats are superior to people in every way. Here's a quick comparison:

PEOPLE	CAT
BODY STRUCTURE	
Have 204 bones.	Has 244 bones.
HEARING	
Contain 6 muscles. Ear cannot pick up important high-frequency notes such as the opening of a refrigerator door.	Contains 30 muscles. This enables the cat to save energy by turning his ear instead of his entire head toward source of sound. Can pick up important high-frequency notes such as the opening of a refrigerator door.
SEEING	
Have difficulty seeing in the dark. Has tendency to bump into things, including each other. Blink often.	Can see in the dark, especially when looking for a midnight snack. Can stare for hours without blinking.

SENSE OF SMELL	
Have only 5 to 20 million olfactory cells and rarely use them for purposes of survival.	Has 67 million olfactory cells and can sniff out a tuna fish sandwich several rooms away.

MUSCULAR COORDINATION	
Poor. Have difficulties climbing up trees and top of dresser.	Excellent. Has no difficulties climbing up trees and top of dresser.

BACKBONE	
Limited in flexibility. Most humans have a problem touching their toes, and some even bending down to tie their shoelaces.	Able to touch his hind legs with the tip of his nose while lying on his back. Tieing shoelaces is no problem; most cats prefer to go barefooted anyway.

COAT	
Coats worn by humans are kept hanging in closets most of the time. Many are hand-me-downs from other animals; i.e., minks, foxes, sables. Most natural hair growth occurs at the top of the head, but even there not always.	Most of the body is covered with fur—his own. Cats are able to make theirs stand on end when facing an enemy; this makes them look bigger and more important.

VOICE	
Rely on polysyllabic words and sentences to get thoughts across. Raising of voice for sustained periods makes it grow hoarse.	Makes fewer sounds but gets point across just the same. As singers, cats excel. Their voices do not grow hoarse, not even after all-night use.

COLORING	
Come only in black, white, yellow and red. No patterns.	Comes in variety of colors. Also in stripes, spots, rosettes, rings, and patches. Coloring often blends into the environment for purposes of camouflage; say, the color of the upholstery or wallpaper.

LIFE EXPECTANCY	
Have only one life.	Has nine lives.

Most owners are
bigger than their cats,
particularly when they stand
on their hind legs.
They assume this position
in an attempt to make
an impression.

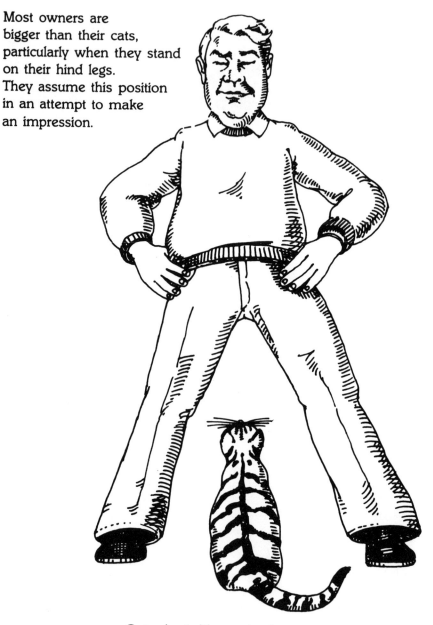

Cats don't like to look *up* to anybody,
and especially not to a human being.

Looking down comes more naturally.

Just like people, cats sometimes feel like climbing the wall.
The difference is that they can do it.

SUMMARY

1) *Felis Domestica* is a misnomer. Cats have yet to be domesticated.

2) Be generous with your cat. Remember: It's better to give than to receive. Ask any cat on the receiving end.

3) Cat's greatest gift to the owner is that he lends you his presence. That should be more than enough.

4) Cats are no bother at all. As long as you feed them right, let them sleep in your bed, scratch their back at their convenience, give them enough room on the living room couch, play with them when they want to, talk to them at length, and spend every waking hour (theirs) with them.

Keeping Your Neurotic Cat Amused 2

For his mental health, if not yours, it is essential that you take time out to play with your cat. This is not necessarily a full-time job; you can stop trying the moment your cat falls asleep.

There are several ways to catch his attention. One is to pretend that you are a cat. Crawl on your hands and knees. Meow. Jump up and down on the couch. Your performance will probably strike your cat as something less than spectacular, but he may still find it amusing enough to stay awake.

Should his interest lag, try something a little more lively. Tell off-color jokes. Sing. Do a tap dance. Open the window, flap your arms, and act as if you were about to take off into the sky. Then live up to your promise. That is sure to excite interest; your cat may even go to the window to see you fly like a bird and land on the ground with a splash.

Cats yawn to let you know how they feel.
Size of gap indicates extent of their boredom.

Cats are proficient at
a number of sporting games:

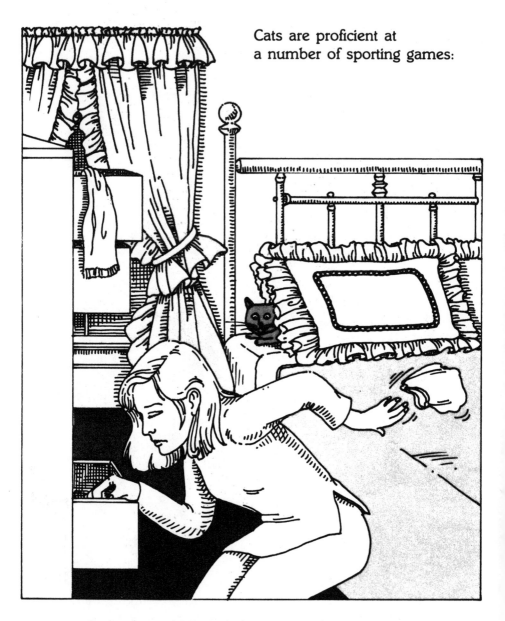

Game One: NOW YOU SEE ME, NOW YOU DON'T

Game Two: I CAN OUTSTARE YOU ANYTIME

Game Three: PILLOW FIGHT

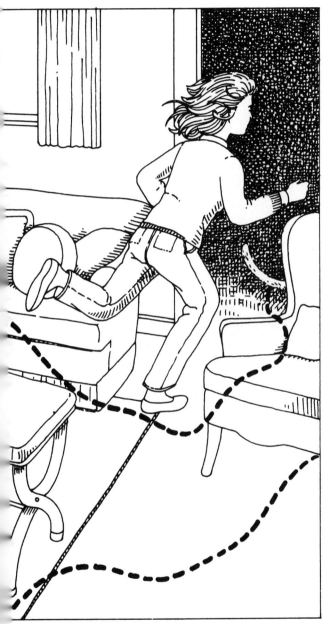

It's not true that cats don't play by the rules. They do as long as they're the ones who make them up. Here are the seven cardinal ones:

1. **Use force**
2. **Confuse**
3. **Cheat**
4. **Lie**
5. **Double-cross**
6. **Bite**
7. **Scratch**

Game Five: TELL ME A STORY

Metamorphoses of the Day. Grandville was also to illustrate the work of the later
and lesser French fabulists Lavalette and Florian (publications of 1841 and 18
His *Robinson Crusoe* illustrations appeared in 1840. The end of th
beginning of a vast undertaking, the first book specifically con
Grandville's genius.

This was one of the two works represented in this
et publique des animaux (Scenes of the Private a
a title which seems to allude to the division of B
Scènes de la vie. An alternate title, used in e
the much altered economical republication of
mêmes et dessinés par un autre (The Anima
Another), which is a clear allusion to the ce
essays and drawings that began publicatio
mêmes (Grandville contributed several i
animal book, which clearly states its im
(Studies of Contemporary Manners). Th
be referred to as *Les Animaux*.

The guiding spirit of the book was
Hetzel (born 1814), who was still w
Paulin, the publisher of the 1835 editi
triumph of wood engraving as a mediur
most of 1840, Hetzel, who enjoyed Gra
work, planned *Les Animaux* as a spotlig
independence for himself. He created the l
of the text under the pseudonym P.-J. Stah
everyone; he was to use it for his original v
wood engravers and sought out many of the n
of the stories (in general, the best) are signed b
Hetzel with some of his. Balzac surely wrote the
consented to the use of her name (perhaps Hetzel
of a plethora of Balzac). This was Balzac's first com
publish a grand illustrated edition of the *Comédie huma*
contributors were the poet and playwright Alfred de Musset, w
choice among thirty-five animal subjects; his brother, Paul de Musset; Ju
novelist and dramatic critic of the *Journal des Débats* for forty-one years; Charles
Nodier, librarian of the Bibliothèque de l'Arsenal, where his literary salon harbored
the great Romantics, and author of numerous tales of dream and fantasy; his tal-
ented daughter Marie Mennessier-Nodier; and Louis Viardot, co-founder of the
important *Revue indépendante*, director of the Théâtre Italien and husband of the
opera singer Pauline Garcia. The other contributors were also writers of much expe-

rience. (In his further career Hetzel published some of the most significant French books of the nineteenth century, his last great author-protégé being Jules Verne.)

many long and elaborate books of the time, *Les Animaux* was issued in bound in colorful paper wrappers. Its hundred installments ember 1840 and ber 1842. The stories were commis-randy gradually during that entire period, ext was supplied to him. The bound clear from the book's subtitle and pref-ment and society (contemporary read-individuals in some of the animal por-ntion). Another claim of the preface, that animals were allowed to speak for nn to name just two well-known writ- of *Les Animaux* with the public is by s correspondence with Hetzel: statu-me being manufactured and sold without stories appear on page 86, together ent-day non-French reader a better idea be understood.

andville's numerous illustrations for *Les Ani-*ous work. For instance, the *Metamorphoses* had -and-bat combination, snakes hissing in a theater, ravens as s nkeys as pain

V

During th achievem dville was pursued by family griefs that affected him y; contem ribe him as gray and stooped at forty. Two ee children her died at the age of four, and she herself 184 is life with her had not been happy, though he dren. She had been overbearing and dictatorial, said to have made curl papers out of drawings by her meet her approval. Certainly his work is deeply tinged with guerite apparently insisted, while on her deathbed, that her husband y again and even appointed her successor, a Mlle. Lhuillier, whom Grandville did marry in 1843 (it seems they had corresponded during Marguerite's lifetime).

One of Grandville's finest jobs of illustration appeared in an 1843 book, *Les petites misères de la vie humaine* (The Petty Sorrows of Human Life). It was in the following year that the publisher-printer Henri Fournier, who had commissioned ville's illustrations for La Fontaine, brought out the book (also represented in

Cats enjoy reading just as much as you, they like the same kind of literature, and are eager to share the experience with you.

Game Six: LET'S MAKE MUSIC TOGETHER

Game Eight: FOLLOW ME

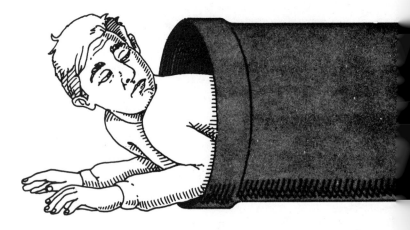

Game Seven: LET'S GO JOGGING

Cats enjoy watching television, especially in the evening after a hard day. The idea of watching others move about on the screen while they can relax appeals to them.

CAT'S GUIDE TO TELEVISION

TYPE OF PROGRAM	OPINION
Football	Too much activity.
Sit-Com	Enjoys most of them, except for the laugh tracks which keep him awake.
Soaps	Takes too much concentration to follow the plot.
Cooking demonstrations	Excellent. Could watch them all day.
Exercise programs	The premise is all wrong.
Cartoons	Good, except "Tom and Jerry."
Love stories	Likes the scenes showing large double beds.
Newscast	Discriminating. They focus on people, not on cats.
"The Tonight Show"	At that hour, everyone should be sleeping, including the host.
Give-away programs	If the prizes are beds and sofas, they're interesting to watch.
Commercials	Time to visit the litter box.

Cats are notoriously sore losers. Coming in second best, especially to someone as poorly coordinated as a human being, grates their sensibility. The only plausible explanation they can think of is that they have actually been *outcheated*—a thought that makes losing an even more traumatic experience.

Should the cat lose, he is likely to remove himself from the scene and head for the bedroom. Here he will probably sit on the corner of the bed, think about the insults he has been made to suffer, and sulk.

Owners often want to know: Should I try reasoning with my depressed cat? Pat him on the head maybe? Give him hope? Kiss him on the forehead and tell him all is not lost? Ask for his forgiveness? The answer is that it all depends on your cat's temper and, most of all, on whether or not he is declawed. Your cat may want to be left alone for a while—a day or two will do it—to sort things out.

All card games bore cats. Except Solitaire.

There are a large variety of toys commercially available for cats. Made of latex, vinyl, rawhide, and other inedible material, they are given to cats with much rejoicing as birthday, Christmas or anniversary presents. They come in the shape of dumbbells, sausages, ladybugs, lollipops, giant balls, peanuts, and even mice. The trouble is that they have been designed by people, not cats. Consequently, cats often choose to ignore these contrivances or let their owners play with them.

Fortunately, the average household is usually well stocked with other toys just right for the cat looking for something to do:

Light switch: It goes on with a flick of a paw.
Clock: Adjust the hands, stop the pendulum.
Toilet bowl: Flush it, listen to it gurgle.
Toilet paper: See how much there is left.
Shower: Turn the faucet, hot or cold.
Soap: Slide it across the floor into the living room.
Dishwasher: Change the switch to "full cycle."
Mop: Eat the spongehead.
Vacuum cleaner: Empty the dustbag, see the dirt fly.
Burglar and smoke alarm: Make it go off, wait for the police and the fire department.
Garbage can: Flip the top, open, strew the dinner on the floor, start picking.
Pressure cooker: Sleep in it.
Food processor: Push the bottom, watch it swirl.
Pillows: Take them to the next room.
Umbrella: Snap it open.
Blow dryer: Watch the hot air escape.
Telephone: Take the receiver off the hook.
Typewriter: Type a letter.
All doors: Open them.

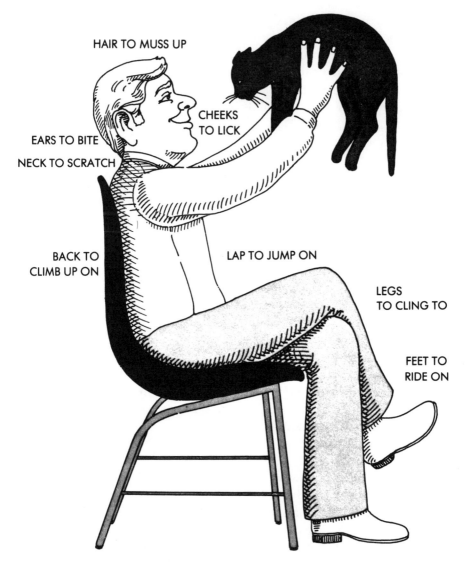

HAIR TO MUSS UP

CHEEKS TO LICK

EARS TO BITE

NECK TO SCRATCH

BACK TO CLIMB UP ON

LAP TO JUMP ON

LEGS TO CLING TO

FEET TO RIDE ON

Of all the toys available, none is better designed than the owner himself. A large multipurpose plaything, its parts can be made to move in almost any direction. It comes completely assembled and it makes a sound when you jump on it.

SUMMARY

1) If your cat doesn't laugh at your joke, try again. You'll get better with practice.

2) Explain the rules to your cat. Then follow his.

3) Don't insist on winning. That'll turn your cat into a loser.

4) Remember: Your cat is not here to entertain you. *You* are here to entertain *him*.

Training the Neurotic Cat | 3

It is said that cats are untrainable. This is not totally accurate. Appearances to the contrary, cats do pay attention to the instructions they receive. They listen closely to what you have to say and sometimes even wait for you to finish your sentence. They understand plain English as well as anybody. How else would it be possible for them to so uncannily do just the opposite?

The problem with most owners is that they don't understand feline psychology. They treat a cat as if he were a *dog*. They issue their order in a loud and commanding voice trying to make up in volume what it lacks in meaning. Should the cat lose his patience and head the other way, they hurl insults at him and use profanity. Some people even resort to chasing their cat up and down the stairs, to the basement or the attic, up to the roof, to the end of the block and out of town, all in hope of making him stop and listen. Still others assert their authority by tossing pillows, shoes, furniture, and telephone directories at the animal. Cats find this type of behavior not only bizarre but a complete waste of energy. There is no record of a moving cat ever being struck by a moving object thrown by a human being, not even by a star pitcher.

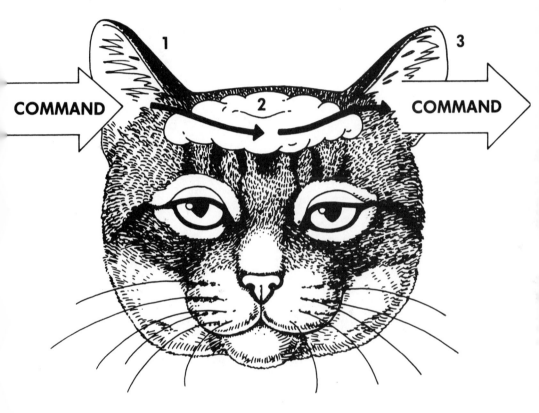

Cat's hearing apparatus is built to allow the human voice to easily go in one ear and out the other. Ear on the left (1) receives command. Sound passes through parts of the brain (2), which discards the message automatically. The sound now is looked upon as a distraction to be eliminated at once. It is made to exit the head with minimum loss to the speed of sound (3). The whole process takes only a few seconds.

Pretentious show of authority may duly impress tigers, lions or other tamed beasts in a circus ring. But not the average house cat, who knows better.

Never scold your cat—especially if he can hear you. If you must shout, lock yourself in the bathroom and do it there. Or, take a walk around the block while mumbling to yourself. The key to successful training is patience, fortitude, and what is known—and well regarded among cats—as Positive Reinforcement.

Positive Reinforcement simply means that you should praise your cat at every turn. This is to build up his self-confidence. Pay him a compliment whether or not he obeyed your command, or—which is more likely—he did just the opposite. Remember that if he failed you, that is all the more reason to bolster his ego. He could be feeling guilty.

Show that you care. Expressions like "what a good cat," "that's a nice kitty, kitty," "well, well, well" go a long way in maintaining communication with your cat.

Scratching his back for one or two hours is even more effective than words alone; it shows that you are willing to make a physical effort to please him.

If you find that neither words nor deeds help you in establishing a rapport with your cat, try appealing to his more basic senses. That means food. Spend some time in the kitchen to prepare his favorite dish. Boil, stew, fry, roast, oven-bake, grill, curry, fricassee, or sauté whatever holds his fancy. Maybe a little garnish will help. Putting the dish in front of him and waving your fingers tells him what it is you would like him to do. Your cat will ignore your orders, of course, but he will show his love for you by eating his reward. Soon you will be able to see the visible result of your efforts; you will now be the owner of a well-rounded cat.

CAT AFTER RECEIVING A MONTH OF POSITIVE REINFORCEMENT TRAINING

BEFORE　　　　**AFTER**

If everything else fails, use body language to get your point across. *Show* him what it is you have in mind.

HOW TO SAY "NO"

Begin your obedience training with the command "no." This should be one of the most important words in your cat's vocabulary. It means the opposite of "yes"—a subtle semantic distinction that frequently escapes cats. For reasons not yet fully understood, the two words tend to sound the same to them.

Since the word "no" has negative connotations, it should be used sparingly, and only in dire emergencies; i.e., your cat wants *all* your bed, your cat has emptied the *entire* refrigerator, your cat has eaten a *whole* bouquet of roses which were sent to you. More than ever, you must pay attention to the tone of your voice. You may want to change the pitch to make the word sound more pleasant to the cat. Remember, cats take pride in their having an ear for music. Like so:

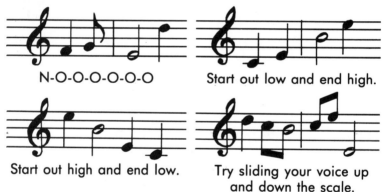

N-O-O-O-O-O-O   Start out low and end high.

Start out high and end low.   Try sliding your voice up and down the scale.

If this doesn't work, repeat the words. Two "no's" are more effective than one; three better than two, and so on. Your chances of being heard will increase with the number of "no's."

If the word "no" offends your cat's sensibilities, try something a bit more subtle. Say "*Please*, no." Or, "Will you please be good enough?" or (if your cat speaks French), "*S'il vous plaît?*"

"COME"

Almost as important as "no" is the word "come." Remember, however, that this calls for an effort on the cat's part so he may want to consider the pros and cons of your proposal before he responds.

Some cats will freeze into a solid mass at the very mention of the word; they find the idea wholly unacceptable or even personally demeaning. Wise cat owners often take advantage of this by using reverse psychology. They say "come" when in fact what they mean is "stay." Conversely, they order their cat to "stay" when they wish him to "come."

The way to make your cat come to you is to give him a reason for doing so. The reason has to be a convincing one; cats are not easily fooled. Try setting a dinner table. If the food smells good, he'll come.

If you find setting a table ten to twenty times a day too demanding, try the string method.

"STAY"

Find out where your cat's favorite sleeping place is. Put him there gently. Keep your hands outstretched with palms up while slowly backing out of the room. All the while, chant "Stay, stay, stay." Walk through the entire house and out the back door into the yard while repeating the command. If you stumble, get back on your feet and move on. Provided the cat is comfortable, he will stay.

"Staying" comes naturally to the cat.

WALKING ON A LEAD

It is not uncommon for owners to take their cats for a stroll around the block. And why not? You must remember, however, that it is a matter of principle with cats that *they lead*. You *follow*.

SITTING UP AND BEGGING

Many owners like to see their cats sit up and beg. For the sake of appearances, some cats will oblige and hold that position for a second or so before toppling over and going back to sleep.

Here's the technique:

STEP ONE:
Place your cat into a fixed upright position.

STEP TWO:
Pull your hands away abruptly. Cats have a natural sense of balance.

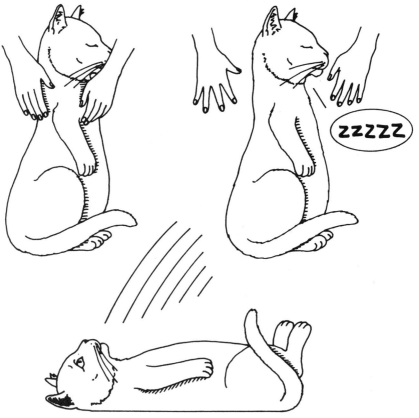

STEP THREE: Now try again.

"SIT"

There are two approaches to teaching your cat to sit. One is to start from a standing position and prevail upon him to sit *down*. The other is to raise him from a prone position and make him sit *up*. The latter is less strenuous for the cat and occurs far more often.

Should you catch your cat in standing position and you want him to sit down, place your hand on his back and push downward. Catch him on his way down.

STEP ONE:
Start at the beginning.

STEP TWO:
Make your cat stand on all fours.

STEP THREE: Now drop the hindquarters. Say " SIT, SIT, SIT."

STEP FOUR:
Now release your cat.

"LIE DOWN"

Lying down is basically nothing more than a logical extension of sitting. He will always respond to this command. He may even comply all on his own.

ADVANCED TRICKS

Now that you know the basics, you—if not your cat—are ready to move on to the next stage. Remember that these are more difficult maneuvers. Expect your cat to take longer to master them.

"SHAKE HANDS"

STEP ONE: Say "Shake."   STEP TWO: Say "Hello there."

STEP THREE: Go through this exercise as long as *your* forepaws hold out.

Cats pick up a wide variety of tricks by watching their older and more accomplished brothers and sisters. This is how wisdom is passed down from one generation to another with truly amazing results.

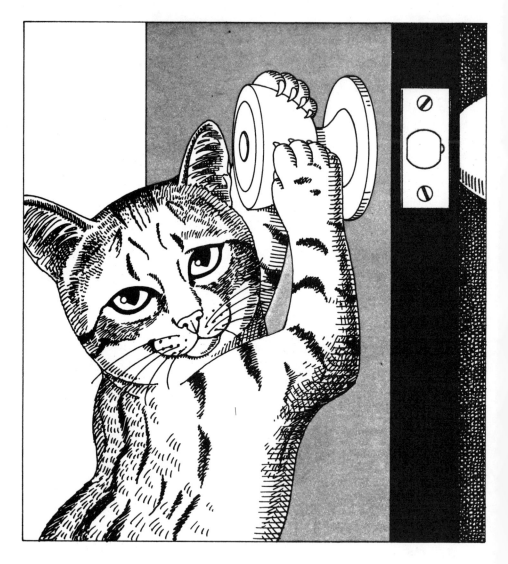

SUMMARY

1) Be nice to your cat.

2) Cats resent too much control. Give them plenty of space. Like the entire living room.

3) Start training your cat at an early age. Cats get set in their ways while still young. Say, an hour or two after birth.

4) The best telephone directory to throw at your cat is the Manhattan White Pages (3½ lbs.).

5) If you don't have a telephone book, use any of the Sears catalogues.

Sleeping Habits of the Neurotic Cat | 4

Owners often complain that their cats sleep all the time. It only seems that way. Your cat may sleep through most of the day, but at night he will stir—especially when he is hungry and decides to head for the kitchen.

The ease with which cats can go to sleep anyplace at any time is truly among the wonders of nature. The phenomenon has long been a source of intrigue with animal behaviorists. Looking for reliable scientific data, they have put cats through a series of controlled experiments. They have dropped them from various heights right side up, upside down, and sideways, in laboratories, in an attempt to wake them up. They have set alarm clocks to go off next to their subjects' ears, jerked their tails, shouted at the top of their lungs, bounced them on trampolines, and exposed them to simulated earthquakes high on the Richter scale. No matter. The results were always the same; the cats never even opened their eyes. The conclusion was that cats had an easier time going to sleep than waking up—an observation that came as no surprise to those who ever owned a cat.

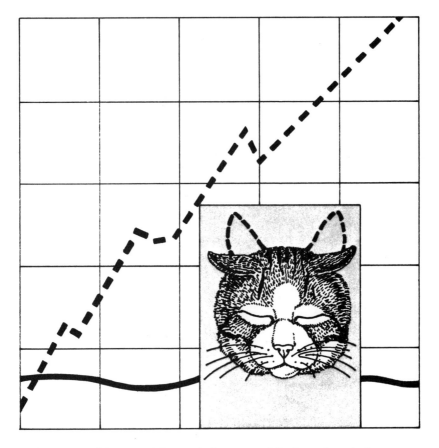

Cats are able to prick up their ears while keeping their eyes firmly closed. This enables them to sleep soundly while appearing to pay attention.

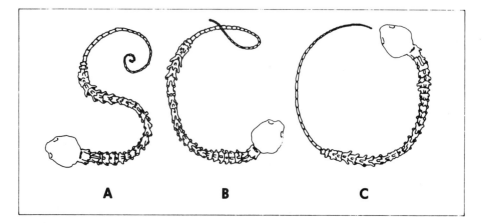

The cat's spinal column is one of the most remarkable parts of his anatomy, an ingenious device that can twist and turn in *any* direction, much like a snake's. Shown here are the (a) S-curve; (b) the semicircle and (c) the full circle. Not shown is the so-called pretzel formation.

A tired cat will always find a place where he can replenish his energy. Some of these may seem uncomfortable to the human eye, but that is only because of our own physical limitations. The flexible backbone allows the cat to fit into any space found in an average home. The more cramped the space, the more suitable.

In fact, the question is often asked: Does a cat possess a genuine backbone? Is he really a member of the vertebrate family (Subphylum Vertebrata) as he pretends or is he faking it? Research provides the answer. X-rays indicate a faint—*very* faint—shadow running down the center of the back. This suggests the presence of some kind of skeleton, and possibly a spinal column. Further research is indicated, just to make sure.

BASIC SLEEPING POSITIONS

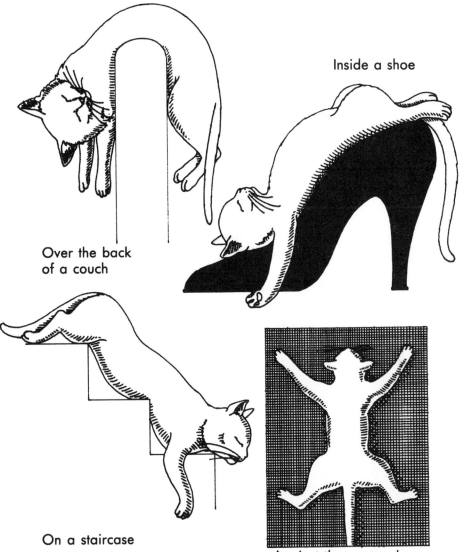

Inside a shoe

Over the back
of a couch

On a staircase

Against the screen door

The bed has a special meaning for the cat. In his opinion this contrivance ranks among the most essential in the house, surpassed only by the refrigerator and the garbage can.

Beds come complete with such amenities as mattresses, pillows, and blankets—and sometimes a human being who takes the place of a hot-water bottle. What's more, beds are usually located in the bedroom where there is privacy. Moreover, he is less likely to be sat upon on the bed than on the living room couch.

Cats don't mind sharing the bed with fellow cats, as long as the area is equitably divided among them. Usually there is room for everyone on a first-come-first-served basis—under the blanket, on top of the blanket, on the pillow, under the pillow, at the head of the bed, at the foot of the bed, in that order. Any space left goes to the owner.

Cats grow in size through the night—or so it seems to the owner who bears up under their weight.

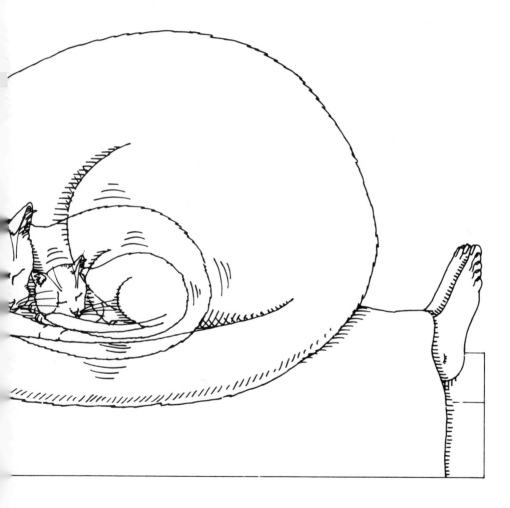

The fact that cats are willing to share the bed with a human being attests to their generous nature. Shown on these pages are the most common types of welcome, and unwelcome, feline sleeping companions.

THE NIGHT WANDERER never stops looking for another spot on the bed promising improvement in comfort. He knows that the shortest distance between two points is a straight line and will never let you forget it.

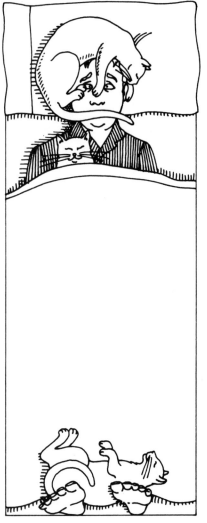 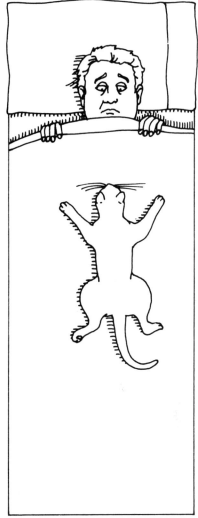

THE SNUGGLER is on a never-ending search for warmth. His favorite resting places include those (1) between the owner's feet, (2) under his armpit, (3) against his face.

THE SOFT-AREA LOVER considers the human belly even softer than the pillow. You must remain in the same position through the night lest you disturb the cat.

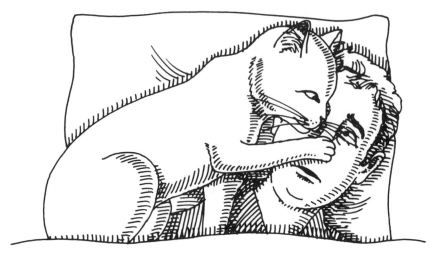

THE HUNTER keeps himself occupied through most of the night tracking down imaginary creatures.

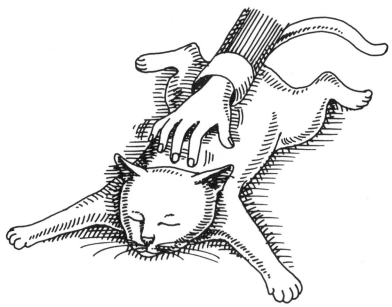

THE ATTENTION SEEKER craves affection.
This cat needs your emotional support—all night long.

THE SERENADER will sing just for you. Always creative, no two songs will ever be alike. Variations in lyrics are "miaw," "meow," and "mew."

THE MIDNIGHT SNACKER is not about to go without food for long periods of time. This cat often knows how to open, but not close, refrigerator doors.

THE FOLLOWER will get up every time you do and will not leave your side for a single moment as you grope your way to the bathroom. He has also been called THE SEEING EYE CAT.

CAT'S EARLY MORNING SCHEDULE

5:30 A.M.   Cat gets up to admire the sunrise from the windowsill.

5:45 A.M.   Cat returns and leaps on your stomach.

6:25 A.M.   Cat glances at the alarm clock.

6:26 A.M.   Cat goes back to sleep.

6:50 A.M.   Alarm clock goes off.

6:51 A.M.   Cat licks your face.

6:55 A.M.   Cat meows.

7:00 A.M.   Cat scratches your ears. You awaken with a start.

THREE-IS-COMPANY is convinced he is wanted.
This cat will be first in bed, last to leave.

DREAM BED is designed to satisfy a cat's basic needs. It consists of (1) a large pillow, (2) foot controls that allow a cat to tilt bed up and down, (3) a bar, (4) giant warm-water bottle replacing human sleeping companion, (5) state-of-the-art stereo equipment, (6) food within paw's reach, (7) remote push-button control television set, (8) "Do Not Disturb" sign, (9) lock, (10) telephone, and (11) a non-working clock.

Cats prefer spring mattresses for maximum comfort.

SUMMARY

1) On the average, cats need 24 hours of sleep a day. Some need more than that.

2) Try not to snore and disturb the cat.

3) Beds designed for pets are all right for dogs or human infants. Cats require *real* beds.

4) Make sure you don't confuse your cat with a bed pillow, even if they do happen to look the same.

5) Don't waste your time shoving your cat off the bed. He will return anyway.

6) Most beds sleep up to six cats. Ten cats without the owner.

How to Feed the Neurotic Cat | 5

The average cat will eat just about anything that we will, and quite a few things that we won't. In fact, there is no term in the English language that adequately describes a cat's eating habits. "Omnivorous" is an obvious understatement. "Multi-omnivorous" hints at the truth, but still fails to explain the cat's versatile palate.

Fortunately, most owners understand the role that a carefully planned diet plays in their cat's physical and emotional well-being. In addition to the usual fare, they provide their cats with such much-needed staples as asparagus, cheese, lobster, bread, pasta, and strawberry shortcake. Knowing better than anybody else what's good for them, cats sometimes complete the menu with houseplants, goldfish, canaries, cigarettes and cigars, crayons, toothpaste, wallpaper, and dirty socks.

Brown bags—something mistakenly referred to as "doggie bags"—for leftovers are furnished by restaurants for people with feelings of guilt about their favorite pets left behind. Cats know their cuisine, however, so be careful about what you bring home.

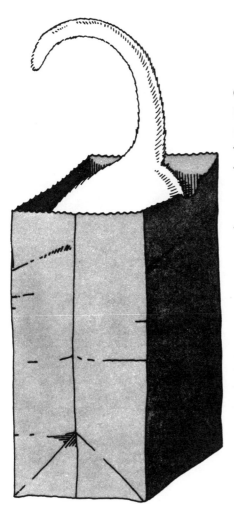

They approve of:

Chez Panisse
La Caravelle
Le Bec-Fin
The Four Seasons
The Palm
Laurent
Lutèce
The Russian Tea Room
L'Hermitage

They do not approve of:

McDonald's
Denny's Donut Shops
Wendy's International
Taco Bell
Howard Johnson's
Dunkin' Donuts
Burger Chef
Burger King

Often overlooked is the fact that cats' taste in food is as finely developed—or probably more so—as humans'.

M·E·N·U

KIBBLES
WATER

Owner's idea of a cat's dinner.

The Four Seasons'

"HOW TO FEED THE NEUROTIC CAT"

Menu

Savory

SQUID SASHIMI

Cold Appetizer

CRABMEAT MOUSSE with BELUGA CAVIAR

Hot Appetizer

SALMON SOUFFLÉ

Intermezzo

TUNA FISH SHERBET

Main Course

STUFFED BABY QUAIL with CRAYFISH TAILS

Dessert

FOIE GRAS TRUFFLES with CRÈME FRAÎCHE

Courtesy of The Four Seasons Restaurant

Cat's idea of dinner.

Mixture of a cat's favorite food items results in a mouth-watering dish commonly known as *Felix Smorgasbord*. This heap of goodies frequently appears in his dreams, causing him to move toward the kitchen promptly upon awakening, or even in his sleep.

Cats have an uncanny knack—some say it borders on the supernatural—to materialize at the dining table the moment food is put on it. They know that, other than the garbage can, this is where food is served at its finest.

The **Chairperson** insists on having his own seat, preferably at the head of the table.

The **Centerpiece** eats at and on the table.
He does not need a plate of his own.

The **Lapcat** shares the plate with the owner
but makes sure he gets the first bite.

Breakfast in Bed shows your thoughtfulness.
Be sure you don't serve it too early;
say, before 2 P.M.

RECOMMENDED:

Hawaiian Fruit Salad
Fried Eggs and Country Sausages
Croissant
Plums in Port Sauce

Sunday Brunch is popular with cats on Sunday, Monday, Tuesday, Wednesday, Thursday, Friday, and Saturday.

Candlelit Dinner ends the day in an appropriate manner. Make sure you don't serve it too late; say after 4 P.M.

RECOMMENDED:

Orange Juice with Champagne
Quiche Lorraine
Salad
Coffee or Tea

RECOMMENDED:

Smithfield Ham
on Honeydew Wedges
Chicken Avgolemono
Crusty French Bread
Chocolate Chiffon Pie
Dry Sauterne

Buffet gives cat a choice of delicacies—
including flowers and candlesticks.

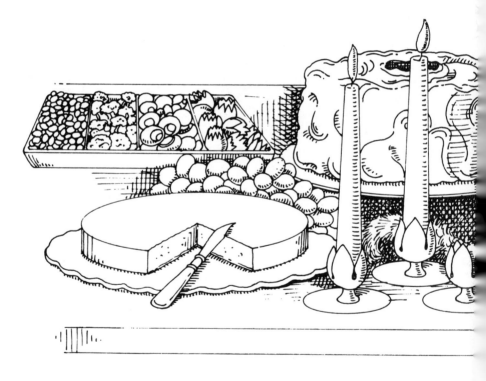

Owners often refuse to admit that their cat has grown too fat for his own good. To spare his feelings, they refer to him as "chubby," "stout," or "stocky"—never obese. But no euphemism can hide the awful truth: a Fat Cat's width often equals his height.

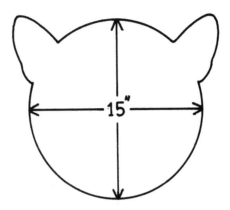

Generally speaking, if your cat no longer fits in a standard-sized bathroom sink, he is fat. If you can't fit him in the bathtub, he is *really* fat.

A common mistake is to confuse the Fat Cat with the Puffed-up Cat. The two look very much alike at a quick glance. The difference is that the Puffed-up Cat makes himself appear bigger by design—and only for given periods of time, as, for example, when he settles down in your armchair and wants to let you know there is room for only one. He accomplishes this amazing change in size by drawing in large amounts of air and holding it until you finally decide to give up and leave.

A good way to reduce your cat's girth is to make him work off the fat. This can be done by putting him through a regular exercise routine, i.e., lifting his paws one at a time, or picking up the entire body and dropping it. Most cats resent force, however. They prefer to rid themselves of calories in their own way and at their own pace. The calorie expenditure table below shows energy expenditures of activities cats normally engage in.

ACTIVITY	CALORIE EXPENDITURE
Jumping up on living room couch	3
Jumping up on top of closet (two tries)	10
Climbing tree (ascend)	25
Climbing tree (descend)	900
Chasing after bird	250
Chasing after dog	100
Being chased by dog	10

Covering distance between living room and kitchen (slow)	5
Covering distance between living room and kitchen (fast)	15
Responding to call (first)	0
Responding to call (second)	0
Responding to call (third)	0
Being pushed off the chair	3
Scratching furniture (painted)	250
Scratching furniture (upholstered)	350
Watching television (same channel)	2
Watching television (changing channels)	5
Rearranging pillows	100
Taking a walk outside (with owner)	20
Taking a walk outside (alone)	2,500
Playing piano	250
Finger painting	110
Misadjusting clock	50
Unscrewing light bulb	350
Moving from one side of bed to other	350
Twitching tail	5

Compact Home Gym makes it possible for cats to remain in their favorite prone position and move parts of their body one at a time with a minimum of effort. **(1)** A lever system raises and lowers forelegs while **(2)** rollers at the opposite end strengthen the hind leg muscles. **(3)** Self-operated shaft is designed to rotate tail protruding through opening. **(4)** Chin band oscillates to eliminate double chin. Attached to **(5)** alarm clock are **(6)** trumpets and **(7)** a siren for sound amplification. The system is especially effective for the cat whose stomach touches the ground as he stands.

SUMMARY

1) Cats need those calories. They may not move around as much as you do, but they expend a lot of energy using their minds.

2) The best place to keep food out of a cat's reach is in your safe, provided he doesn't know the combination.

3) Cats are vegetarians, too. They eat houseplants.

4) Cats do not like the word "refuse" for leftovers. They have never refused anything edible, semi-edible, or un-edible.

Grooming the Neurotic Cat | 6

Most cats are quite content with the way they look. In their mind, there's not much room for improvement. Unfortunately, not all owners share that opinion. Many have their own notions of feline beauty. Some even go as far as to attempt to give their cat a bath—the ultimate confrontation between Man and Cat.

Cats' objections to taking baths are not based on philosophical grounds only. They know that such an approach to hygiene not only represents inefficient use of their time and everyone else's, but lacks all reason. Unlike people, cats wash themselves several times a day.

To bathe a cat takes brute force, perseverance, courage of conviction—and a cat. The last ingredient is usually the hardest to come by. As adept as cats are in making a prompt appearance at dinnertime, so they are at vanishing at even the vaguest prospect of having to take a bath.

Shown on these pages are the basic steps involved in giving your cat a bath.

STEP ONE: Put on strong, waterproof apron or a wet suit complete with face mask, or, if available, armor.

STEP TWO: Fill about half the sink with water. Cat will fill up rest of space.

STEP THREE: Take a deep breath.

STEP FOUR: Now go and look for cat.

STEP FIVE: Find cat.

STEP SIX: Take cat to the sink.

STEP SEVEN: Now wash the cat. Try keeping him in the sink for several minutes. Wash all parts: (1) face, (2) paws, (3) tail. You will need soap; use it before he eats it.

STEP EIGHT: Should your cat pry himself loose, don't give up.
Track him down. Just follow the wet pawmarks.

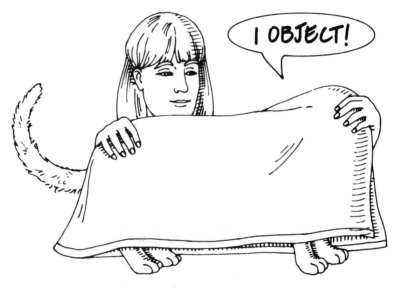

STEP NINE: Ignore his objections and dry him vigorously.

STEP TEN: Take care of your injuries.

Cats have mixed feelings about grooming. They are against it on principle; the implication is clear that someone thinks their appearance is less than perfect. They will, however, submit to brushing, especially when the brushes you use are designed especially for them. Here they are:

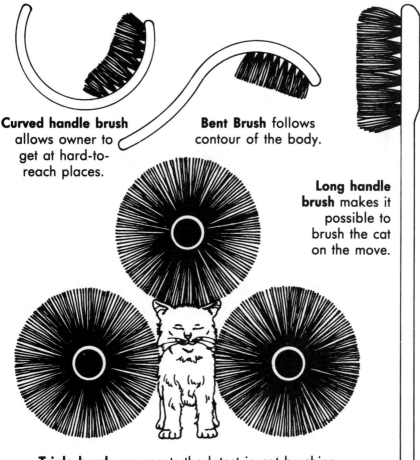

Curved handle brush allows owner to get at hard-to-reach places.

Bent Brush follows contour of the body.

Long handle brush makes it possible to brush the cat on the move.

Triple brush represents the latest in cat brushing. Inspired by the technology used in the automatic car wash, the system is fast and efficient.

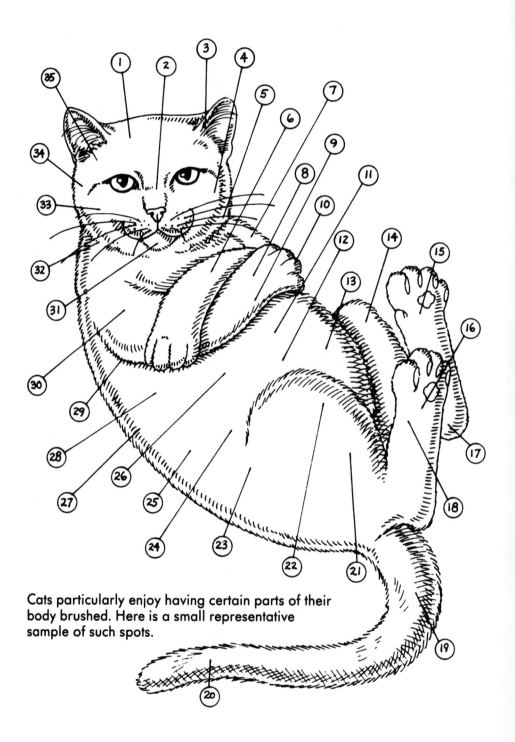

Cats particularly enjoy having certain parts of their body brushed. Here is a small representative sample of such spots.

SUMMARY

1) Have plenty of large towels handy when you bathe a cat. You will need them to dry yourself off.

2) Do not use ammonia, turpentine, or paint remover when washing your cat, much as you may be tempted to.

3) Do not put your cat in the washing machine, much as you may be tempted to.

4) Do not flush your cat down the toilet, much as you may be tempted to.

5) Remember: It is ducks who take to water, *not* cats.

Your Dog and the Neurotic Cat | 7

Cats don't object to living under the same roof with a dog as long as it is clearly understood that it is the cat who gets the easy chair, the bed, the television set, and all the sun spots on the carpet.

From the cat's point of view, such an arrangement is eminently fair. Remember that he has already given up much of his territory to someone else in the household, namely you.

Consider, too, that dogs are different from cats. From the very beginning, dogs set out to please their masters, not the other way around. And so they became "Man's Best Friend." The title holds absolutely no appeal to the cat.

History proves that dogs' insistence on loyalty and devotion makes their life more difficult, not easier. They were put to work to perform a wide variety of chores. And so today's canine community is broken up into such groups as hunting dogs, shepherd dogs, military dogs, racing dogs, watchdogs, circus dogs, draught dogs, and truffle dogs. Of the ninety-six major canine breeds, only sixteen are defined as "pet dogs." Not so with cats. All go under the banner of "pet," a word the dictionary defines as "any loved and cherished creature," an excellent choice of words from the cat's point of view.

I AM WHAT I AM.

Unlike dogs, cats have never agreed to changing their appearance only to please their breeders.

Dogs travel hundreds of miles during their lifetime, responding to such commands as "come" and "fetch." Cats approach people only when there is a reason, and not always even then.

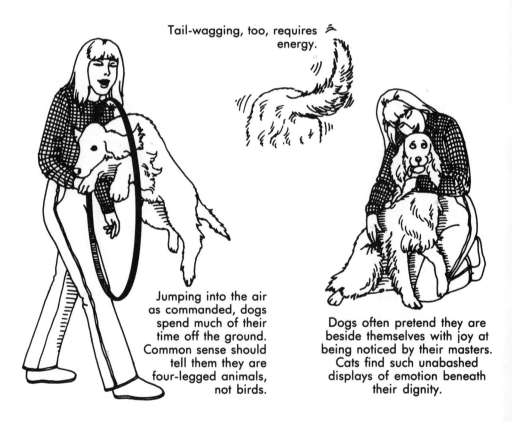

Tail-wagging, too, requires energy.

Jumping into the air as commanded, dogs spend much of their time off the ground. Common sense should tell them they are four-legged animals, not birds.

Dogs often pretend they are beside themselves with joy at being noticed by their masters. Cats find such unabashed displays of emotion beneath their dignity.

In trying to look good, a dog ends up making a fool of himself. He does what is expected of him and becomes a yes-dog in the process. There are *no* yes-cats.

Any cat knows that he has it all over dogs, both physically and mentally. Here is a chart to prove the point.

DOG	CAT
Must go outdoors to relieve himself on fire hydrants, tree trunks, tires of parked cars.	Uses litter box as his own private bathroom right at home.
Will follow orders.	Will not follow orders.
Whines when owner leaves house.	Will calmly go to sleep when owner leaves house.
Cannot cling to screen doors.	Can cling to screen doors.
Cannot climb up draperies.	Can climb up draperies.
Always the same basic shape.	Can change shape to fit into any odd space.
Cannot use the typewriter.	Can use the typewriter.
Cannot play the piano.	Can play the piano.
Howls.	Sings.
Will keep quiet when so ordered.	Will make *more* noise when asked to be quiet.
Bites but doesn't scratch.	Bites *and* scratches.
Looks guilty when reprimanded.	Looks the same when reprimanded.
Smiles to please.	Keeps a straight face no matter what.

Cat's athletic prowess allows him to jump over dog's head.
Dog soon stops trying.

In any paw-to-paw battle, the cat wins easily.
Shown here is cat persuading dog to switch to a different television program.

Still, dogs do serve a useful purpose.

SUMMARY

1) Dogs may be bigger than cats. But not between the ears.

2) If your dog and cat don't get along, talk to your dog. He is the only one who will listen.

3) If your home is not big enough for both your dog and cat, you have two choices. Get rid of the dog. Or move into a bigger home.

How to Analyze Your Neurotic Cat at Home

8

Professional counseling can be expensive, especially if both the owner and the cat must undergo treatment. Therefore, many cat owners choose to psychoanalyze their pet at home instead of at a therapist's office. This is not as difficult as it sounds. All that's required is a living room couch, you, and the cat. Tranquilizers may come in handy if you're the nervous type.

To be successful in your analysis of your cat, you must first of all understand him. Ask yourself: What makes your cat act the way he does?

There are two likely possibilities: you and/or the food you serve. Having explored these two areas, you may then proceed to examine other more complex causes: a dog in the house, a newly arrived baby, another cat.

Stay with the therapy as long as necessary. You cannot expect to change deeply ingrained habits overnight. In ten or fifteen years you will begin to see some changes, if not in your cat, then in yourself.

Cat's position on the couch tells much about his underlying personality conflicts. Head buried in your chest indicates basic insecurity.

This pose is typical of a cat with a fixation; in this case, your knee. Try unfastening him by lifting one claw at a time. If that doesn't work, walk around the room.

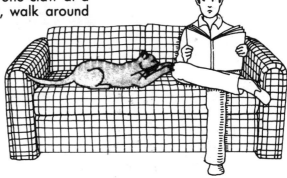

This cat has no use for therapy. He is a well-adjusted cat.

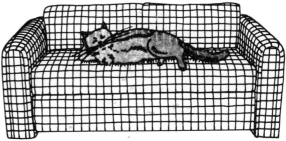

If you have more than one cat, try group therapy.
A permissive atmosphere will encourage your subjects
to act out their basic hostilities.

FELINE NORMALCY TEST

Answers to these questions will help you to decide whether or not your cat is in need of therapy.

Does your cat:

	YES	NO
(1) sleep less than three hours at any one time?	☐	☐
(2) stay at the same spot on your bed for more than 10 minutes?	☐	☐
(3) refuse to come to the dinner table?	☐	☐
(4) keep quiet when you ask him to?	☐	☐
(5) get up in the morning at the sound of the alarm clock?	☐	☐
(6) respond to his name?	☐	☐
(7) pay attention to *anything* being said?	☐	☐
(8) stay on low ground when he has a chance to leave it for a higher place?	☐	☐
(9) observe goldfish rather than eating them?	☐	☐
(10) sleep in his own bed?	☐	☐
(11) walk around a flower bed instead of crossing through it?	☐	☐
(12) pass a mirror without taking a peek at his image?	☐	☐
(13) let you walk out the door before him?	☐	☐

(14) sit still when you want to take his photograph? ☐ ☐

(15) not jump in your lap when you sit down? ☐ ☐

(16) prefer to stay home in the evenings when he has a chance to go out and have a good time? ☐ ☐

(17) prefer to listen to you instead of television? ☐ ☐

(18) respect your dog? ☐ ☐

(19) prefer his own food over yours? ☐ ☐

(20) obey commands? ☐ ☐

If your answer is "yes" to any of the above questions, he is in serious need of immediate psychiatric attention.

Picture of a normal cat

Reflex Reaction Test can be given in your home. Stepping on your cat's tail will start him climbing up your draperies. A physically fit and emotionally well-adjusted cat should be able to cover a distance of 10 feet in less than 3 seconds.

Depth Perception Test helps you to evaluate your cat's ability to judge distances between such given points as **(1)** top of chest, **(2)** floor, **(3)** top of bed, and **(4)** top of your head.

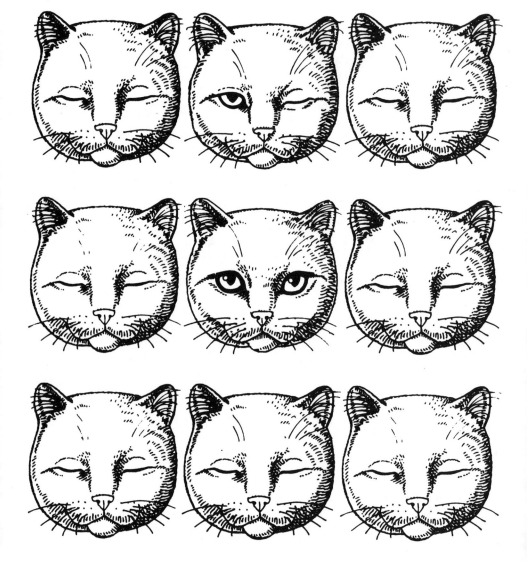

Alertness Test tells about your cat's alertness, if any. All cats fall into one of the types shown here. Watch for eye movements. They could be the only sign of activity.

Alert Cat opens one eye if you are shouting loud enough. He will keep it open for several seconds.

Exceptionally Alert Cat opens both eyes when you talk to him. He will wait for you to finish before closing time.

Average Cat does not open his eyes at all.

HOSTILITY FACTOR

Cats usually keep their opinions to themselves in order to avoid getting into a needless argument with a person bigger than they are. Bottling up their feelings, however, puts additional stress on their already overstressed nervous system. Understanding the causes of their frustration—and perhaps doing away with them—will aid you in dealing with your cat.

Here's a list* of the cat's favorite Hate Objects:

All people except the owner
All people including the owner
Small dogs
Large dogs
Dog lovers
Parakeets
Canaries
Hamsters
Mice
All cats except himself
Overcooked hamburgers
Frozen TV dinners
Rocking chairs
Veterinarians
Rain

Garbage cans with sealed tops
Door locks
Storm windows
Birds that get away
Claw clippers
Owners who take vacations
Carrying containers
Alarm clocks
Closed drawers
Hammocks
Water beds
Cat food commercials
The proverb "There's more than one way to skin a cat"

*This is only a partial list.

ATTENTION SPAN

ACTIVITY	ATTENTION SPAN
Being called	2 seconds
Being called by name	2 seconds
Being told to go somewhere else	None
Being told to go somewhere else in loud voice	None
Smell of fillet of sole wafting across living room	Half hour
Dog barking	5 seconds
Dog barking at the cat	2 seconds
Owner unmaking bed to retire	10 minutes
Birds outside the window	1 hour
Pat on the back	2 seconds
Scratching between the ears	5 hours
Half-hour TV program	half hour (minus commercials)
Owner unpacking groceries	10 minutes
Owner putting food in refrigerator	10 minutes
Owner getting out of bed in the morning before cat does	None
Owner leaving home	1 second
Owner returning home with bag of groceries	15 seconds

Ability to show affection.
Rumor has it that cats are aloof and undemonstrative.
This is not so. Cats do return affection in kind.

Now at last you **understand** your cat.

SUMMARY

1) Cats are not born neurotic. They usually become so a few minutes after birth.

2) Don't waste your money on professional psychiatric fees for your cat. You will need it for your own analysis.

3) Don't waste your time analyzing your cat's guilt feelings. He doesn't have any.

4) Don't be alarmed if your cat seems abnormal. It's normal for cats to be that way.

Can the Neurotic Cat Be Cured? | 9

No.